D1198911

SEP 2002

3/07

SHERYL SWOOPES

A Real-Life Reader Biography

John Torres

Mitchell Lane Publishers, Inc.

P.O. Box 619
Bear, Delaware 19701

Mitchell Lane
PUBLISHERS

First Printing

Real-Life Reader Biographies

Selena	Robert Rodriguez	Mariah Carey	Rafael Palmeiro
Tommy Nuñez	Trent Dimas	Cristina Saralegui	Andres Galarraga
Oscar De La Hoya	Gloria Estefan	Jimmy Smits	Mary Joe Fernandez
Cesar Chavez	Chuck Norris	Sinbad	Paula Abdul
Vanessa Williams	Celine Dion	Mia Hamm	Sammy Sosa
Brandy	Michelle Kwan	Rosie O'Donnell	Shania Twain
Garth Brooks	Jeff Gordon	Mark McGwire	Salma Hayek
Sheila E.	Hollywood Hogan	Ricky Martin	Britney Spears
Arnold Schwarzenegger	Jennifer Lopez	Kobe Bryant	Derek Jeter
Steve Jobs	Sandra Bullock	Julia Roberts	Robin Williams
Jennifer Love Hewitt	Keri Russell	Sarah Michelle Gellar	Liv Tyler
Melissa Joan Hart	Drew Barrymore	Alicia Silverstone	Katie Holmes
Winona Ryder	Alyssa Milano	Freddie Prinze, Jr.	Enrique Iglesias
Christina Aguilera	Marc Anthony	Cheech Marin	Shakira
Jessica Simpson	Mandy Moore	Tiger Woods	**Sheryl Swoopes**
Bruce Lee	Gary Paulsen	J.K. Rowling	Roald Dahl
Dr. Seuss	Christopher Paul Curtis	Maurice Sendak	

Library of Congress Cataloging-in-Publication Data
Torres, John Albert.
        Sheryl Swoopes/John Torres.
            p. cm.— (A real-life reader biography)
        Includes index.
        ISBN 1-58415-068-8
        1. Swoopes, Sheryl—Juvenile literature. 2. Basketball players—United States—Biography—Juvenile literature.
3. Women basketball players—United States—Biography—Juvenile literature. [1. Swoopes, Sheryl. 2. Basketball
players. 3. Women—Biography. 4. African Americans—Biography.] I. Title. II. Series.
GV884.S88 T67 2001
796.323'092—dc21
[B]
00-067805

ABOUT THE AUTHOR: John A. Torres is a newspaper reporter for the Poughkeepsie Journal in New York. He has written eleven sports biographies, including *Greg Maddux* (Lerner), *Hakeem Olajuwon* (Enslow), and *Darryl Strawberry* (Enslow). He lives in Fishkill, New York with his wife and two children. When not writing, John likes to spend his time fishing, coaching Little League baseball, and spending time with his family.

DEDICATION: This book is dedicated to my daughter, Scout, who has dreams as big as the mountains and the heart to match.

PHOTO CREDITS: cover: Ronald Martinez/Allsport; p. 4 Allsport; p. 7 Archive Photos; p. 19 Globe Photos; p. 27 Marin & Associates; p. 28 The Sporting Image; p. 29 Allsport; p. 30 Archive Photos.

ACKNOWLEDGMENTS: The following story has been thoroughly researched, and to the best of our knowledge, represents a true story. While every possible effort has been made to ensure accuracy, the publisher will not assume liability for damages caused by inaccuracies in the data, and makes no warranty on the accuracy of the information contained herein. This story has not been authorized nor endorsed by Sheryl Swoopes.

Table of Contents

Chapter 1
Gold

It was the moment that Sheryl Swoopes had waited for and worked for and dreamed about her entire life. Along with her teammates on the United States Women's Olympic basketball team, Sheryl was about to play for the ultimate goal: a gold medal in women's basketball.

The 1996 Summer Olympics, held in Atlanta, Georgia, became a showcase for the 12 women known as Team USA who were out to prove that they were the world's best women's basketball team.

Team USA set out to prove they were the world's best women's basketball team.

They had been practicing and playing together for more than 14 months. During that time, they had played 52 games against some of the best college teams in the country as well as top foreign teams and won all of them. In the Olympics, they won seven more games to qualify for the gold medal game. This was quite an accomplishment and newspapers everywhere were saying that this American group was the best women's basketball team ever.

But their opponent, the Brazilian National Team, was also undefeated in the Olympic tournament. It would not be an easy game.

Sheryl was clearly one of the team's leaders, using her deadly outside shooting to make 60 percent of her shots and average 13 points. In addition, she pulled down nearly four rebounds in every game and added four assists, where she helped a teammate to score a basket by passing the ball to her.

And she also led by example. Sheryl was one of the hardest workers on the team, never letting up during practice or games — no matter what the score was.

Not only that, Sheryl proved her leadership through her toughness. International basketball is a lot more physical than American women are used to playing. The athletes are bigger and use a more bruising style of play, especially close to the basket where Sheryl would often drive to the hoop. Things that American referees

Sheryl partici-pated in both the 1996 and 2000 Summer Olym-pics. Here is Sheryl (left) at the gold medal match in Sydney, Aus-tralia, September 30, 2000.

Sheryl's dream of winning a gold medal came true.

would whistle as fouls are accepted as part of the international game.

But Sheryl never complained. She took the hacks that opposing players gave her and kept playing. Actually, years of playing basketball with her physical older brothers probably helped her a great deal.

Still another part of Sheryl's game, which her teammates never overlooked, was her defense. She worked just as hard when the other team had the ball. Her specialty was stealing the ball in the backcourt from the player she was guarding and then driving to the basket for an easy lay-in.

The gold medal game was close for a while. But with the rowdy, supportive crowd that kept chanting "U-S-A, U-S-A," Sheryl's shooting and the rebounding of Rebecca Lobo and Lisa Leslie, the Americans pulled away in the second half to win easily by the score of 111-87.

Sheryl's dream of winning a gold medal had come true. Talent, hard work, and dedication had all paid off.

There were tears in her eyes as she stood with her teammates and received her gold medal while the national anthem played. The feeling went beyond just proving to the world that she was part of the best basketball team. Sheryl felt as if she won the medal both for herself and for her country.

Little did Sheryl and her teammates know that their Olympic performance, their great play, their gold medal against international competition, would change the face of women's basketball.

Sheryl Swoopes, the 6-foot, 145-pound shooting guard, had certainly come a long way from a Texas playground where the boys would never let her play basketball. And the best was yet to come.

Sheryl and her teammates did not know that their Olympic perfor—mance would change the face of women's basketball.

Chapter 2
Growing Up

"We grew up in a three room house," Sheryl said.

Sheryl Denise Swoopes was born on March 25, 1971 in Brownfield, Texas, a town with a population of about 10,000 people. It's in a relatively poor area known for oil, wheat — and tornadoes!

Times were tough growing up in the Swoopes household. Her father left the family when Sheryl was very young. That meant that her mother, Louise, had to raise Sheryl and her three brothers all by herself.

"We grew up in a three-room house," Sheryl said. "Not three bedrooms. Three rooms."

Money was tight so Louise had to work two jobs. It took a lot of work and a lot of love on her part to keep the family together — and fed.

The family did not have enough money to buy a real basketball hoop so they had to use an old bicycle wheel attached to an old piece of wood that was nailed to the back of the house.

Even though her children loved basketball, Louise made sure that there were no games played until daily homework and chores were done. She would constantly stress to her children the importance of getting a good education.

It's no wonder that to this day Sheryl considers her mother as her hero.

You could almost say that Sheryl grew up on a basketball court since she spent most of her childhood following her older brothers, James and Earl, when they went to play basketball. When she was too young to play, Sheryl would pretend to be a cheerleader and

The family did not have enough money to buy a real basketball hoop.

make up chants and cheers while watching them.

When she grew a little bit older, Sheryl was not content with being a cheerleader. She wanted to play. But her brothers told her basketball was a sport just for boys. Sheryl did not give up. She soon began dribbling the basketball whenever she had free time and she kept following them to the backyard or to the neighborhood basketball court. Whenever no one was using the basket, she would spend her time shooting.

She would hang around the courts and whenever a team was short one player they would ask her to play. Her dribbling skills and her speed were astonishing. Not only was Sheryl able to hold her own with the boys, she was actually better than a lot of them.

She was such a good dribbler that sometimes she would tease the boys and dare them to try to steal the ball away from her. She would dribble through her legs, behind her back and very low to the ground. These little games would

Sheryl's brothers told her that basketball was a sport just for boys.

prove valuable to Sheryl later on in her career.

"Once you go out and play with guys, you figure you can always score off girls," Sheryl said.

Her mother, Louise, recognized what a natural Sheryl seemed to be on the court. So when Sheryl was eight years old her mother signed her up on a girls' basketball team called the Little Dribblers. Sheryl had become so good and so tough playing with her older brothers and the boys on the local courts that she simply dominated the league.

Her teammates started calling Sheryl "Legs" because of her dribbling skills and her long legs on the basketball court.

When she was nine Sheryl led the Little Dribblers team to the national championship tournament in Beaumont, Texas. Louise scrimped and saved and was able to take the entire family to go watch Sheryl participate. It was the first vacation they had ever taken together.

Sheryl's mother realized she had natural talent and signed her up for a girl's team called the Little Dribblers.

Sheryl soon realized there was a place for her on the court.

Sheryl did not disappoint them. She dominated the tournament with her speed and her great dribbling skills. She led her team to the final game of the tournament but the opposing team was just too powerful. Though the Little Dribblers were finally defeated in the tight championship game, Sheryl's confidence grew to new heights. Now she knew that basketball was not only for boys. Now she knew that there was a place for her on the court.

Chapter 3
Don't Give Up

Growing up with an intense love of sports, Sheryl was frustrated that throughout junior high school she was forced to be a spectator and watch the boys play. Her school had no girls' teams. She knew she was good enough to represent the school too and felt cheated. She would have to wait until high school to participate in school sports.

But that didn't stop Sheryl from playing basketball and from working hard to be a better player. During the summer she would go down to the high school gymnasium and practice. She

In junior high, there was no girls' basketball team so Sheryl just had to watch the boys.

would play alone or with the boys from the high school team. Most of them became friends with her and would always let her play. But one or two always gave her a hard time and told her that basketball was a boys' sport. Sometimes they were so mean that they made Sheryl cry. She even thought about quitting.

But Sheryl's friends along with her mother convinced her not to give up. They knew how good Sheryl was and they told her that she would have a good shot at making the junior varsity basketball team when she got to high school.

Boy, were they wrong!

Sheryl did not make the junior varsity team when she enrolled at Brownfield High School. She made the varsity, which is usually made up of 12th graders and maybe a lucky 11th grader or two. Sheryl was only in 9th grade and was already on the team.

And she didn't limit herself to basketball. Now that she was in high school, Sheryl discovered that she loved to compete in many sports. As a natural athlete Sheryl excelled in everything she tried.

Her speed and agility made her an asset to the school's track and field team. She set several records — often breaking her own — in the long jump in addition to being a good sprinter. She also was a star volleyball player because of her height, jumping ability, and coordination.

But it was basketball that Sheryl loved the most. She played a lot as a freshman and earned a starting position as a sophomore. By the time Sheryl was a junior, it was her team. She led the other players by her hard work, good grades, and never-say-die attitude on the basketball court.

That year she led the Brownfield Lady Cubs basketball team to the state championship and was named the player of the year in Texas. Recruiters, scouts, and coaches attended most of her games as a junior and began

When she was a junior, she led her basketball team to the state champion–ship.

watching her every move. So even before Sheryl entered her senior year, it was obvious she would earn a basketball scholarship to just about any major college in the country she wanted. By being such a great basketball player, Sheryl would be able to go to school for free.

As a senior, she averaged 26 points, 5 assists, and 14 rebounds per game. She was named All-American.

When she was a senior, she was named All-American.

But Sheryl wanted to remain close to home. So she accepted a full-tuition scholarship to the University of Texas, where the Lady Longhorns enjoyed a great reputation as one of the most powerful basketball teams in the country. Sheryl would surely have the chance to shine on a national stage, not just in Texas.

But when Sheryl left the small town of Brownfield for the big-city life of Austin where the University of Texas is located, she became intimidated by the big crowds and the big buildings.

She became homesick right away, missing her family and friends and small town life where everybody knew everybody else. After one week she quit the school and flew home to Brownfield.

Once again her family and friends told her not to give up. So she enrolled at South Plains Community College, a two-year school just 30 miles from Brownfield, where she could take classes and play basketball. It certainly would not be on the same level as a Division I school like the University of Texas, but it was better than nothing.

Sheryl at the American Sports Awards in 1994.

Sheryl made an immediate impact at South Plains Community College. It was obvious from the minute she stepped onto the basketball court that Sheryl did not belong there. She was too good and simply dominated the competition. She led what had been known as an average team to a 27-9 record and was named junior college All-American during her first year.

Her sophomore season was even better. She led the team to a 25-4 record, was named the most valuable player of the Western Junior College Conference, and set 28 new conference records,

At South Plains Community College, Sheryl made an immediate impact.

including most points in a game with 45 and 139 steals during her sophomore season.

Sheryl had helped put the small junior college "on the map." Now she wanted to earn her four-year college degree and continue playing basketball close to home against Division I competition to see just how good she was. It was time to help put another lesser-known school "on the map."

So she enrolled at Texas Tech University, a Division I school that seemed to always finish behind the University of Texas in most sports — especially women's basketball. Like South Plains, Texas Tech was only about 30 miles from Sheryl's home.

In Sheryl's first year at the college, the team finished with a 27-5 mark. The fans loved watching her aggressive style of play and often chanted "Swoopes, Swoopes" during games. The team won the Southwest Conference championship and was invited to the NCAA tournament. This annual

At Texas Tech, Sheryl led her team to the Southwest Conference champion-ship.

tournament pits college's best teams against each other to determine the national champion.

The Texas Tech Lady Raiders made it all the way to the West Regional semifinals before being eliminated. But Sheryl was already having a positive effect on the basketball program as high school girls suddenly expressed an interest in playing for the Lady Raiders.

Her coach, Marsha Sharp, knew how important Sheryl was to the team.

"We can compete on a national level because of her," Sharp said. "She'll be a legend in women's basketball, but not just because of her play. She has the charisma that the crowd loves."

After the season, Sheryl started training hard in order to make the 1992 U.S. Olympic basketball team. She was hoping to compete during the summer and then return to Texas Tech for her final season. But she injured her knee, which required minor surgery. That ended her 1992 Olympic dream but she

Sheryl was not able to compete in the 1992 Summer Olympics because she injured her knee.

would be okay for her final year at Texas Tech.

Sheryl's senior year at Texas Tech would prove to be one of the most incredible single seasons for a woman college basketball player — ever. She averaged 26 points per game during the regular season as the Lady Raiders rolled to a 31-3 record. But like most great champions, Sheryl almost seemed to hold back, waiting to play her best during the conference tournament and the NCAA tournament.

In the Southwest Conference championship game, the Lady Raiders faced off against the University of Texas — where Sheryl had gone to school for about a week before getting homesick. Sheryl was unstoppable. She poured in 53 points to lead the Lady Raiders to a 78-71 victory. It was the most points scored by a woman that season.

Sheryl was set now for the NCAA tournament and her goal was to bring the college championship to Texas Tech. The Lady Raiders breezed by their first

In her senior year, Sheryl was set to bring the NCAA tournament champion-ship to Texas Tech.

three opponents, Washington, Southern California, and Colorado to make it to the Final Four.

Sheryl put on a one-woman show against top-ranked Vanderbilt in the semi-final matchup, scoring 31 points and grabbing 11 rebounds as her team cruised to a 60-46 victory. And Sheryl was saving her best for last.

In the final game, Texas Tech squared off against basketball powerhouse Ohio State. It was more like Sheryl's personal stage. She scored 47 points, which included four three-point shots, to pull her team to a tough 84-82 victory and the national title. That was the most points that any player, male or female, had ever scored in a Division I championship game.

Ohio State's head coach, Nancy Darsch paid Sheryl the ultimate compliment afterward.

"You don't appreciate Sheryl Swoopes until you have to try and stop her," she said.

"You don't appreciate Sheryl Swoopes until you have to try and stop her."

Chapter 5
Life After College

Sheryl had won just about every major college award there was. She had led her team to the college championship and she hurdled every obstacle in her way. But after graduating from Texas Tech Sheryl faced another challenge. There was almost nowhere for her to play.

Men have several professional basketball options after finishing their college careers but for women the pickings were slim. Finally, a professional team in Italy offered Sheryl a contract. She did not want to be so far from home and her family but there

Sheryl won about every major college award there was.

were really no other options. Sheryl accepted and flew to Italy.

She played well there for about three months before she was just too homesick. Sheryl flew home, took a job as a bank teller and played in pickup games at night. She also began to deliver radio commentary on women's athletics. During this time Sheryl married her high school sweetheart Eric Jackson.

But a few months later, Sheryl was invited to be part of an American amateur team that would start playing in international tournaments. She also met her idol, Michael Jordan, and the two even got to play some one-on-one basketball.

"One dream of mine was to someday meet Michael Jordan," Sheryl said. "He was my role model, someone that I admire on and off the court. I used to tell my friends that someday I would meet him."

Performing well in these tournaments and her exposure after

After college, Sheryl accepted an offer to play basketball in Italy.

playing Michael Jordan made Sheryl the most recognizable woman basketball player in the country. Her face began appearing in commercials and even on a box of Kellogg's Corn Flakes. In 1995 Nike decided to introduce a line of women's basketball shoes.

Sheryl saw one of her biggest dreams come true when two pro women's basketball leagues were started in the United States.

"I was speechless," Sheryl said when Nike called her with their plans for the new "Air Swoopes" shoes. "At first I thought they were joking. Then I cried. I thought I was dreaming."

But it wasn't a dream. She was the first woman to have shoes named after her.

And soon afterward, another dream came true.

After the gold medal victory in 1996 proved how popular women's basketball had become, two professional leagues were formed in the United States. There was the American Basketball League (ABL) and the Women's National Basketball Association (WNBA).

Sheryl liked the fact that the WNBA would let her play for a team in her home state of Texas.

Both leagues wanted Sheryl to be their star attraction, but the WNBA

promised Sheryl she could play for a team in her home state of Texas. So in 1997 Sheryl became the first player chosen by the Houston Comets. However, the season would have to start without her. Sheryl was doing something more important.

In June, Sheryl and her husband became the parents of a little boy they would name Jordan — after Sheryl's idol.

Sheryl began playing not long afterward and her professional career has been a continuation of her tremendous college and amateur accomplishments. She has helped lead the Comets to several WNBA titles while compiling a career scoring average of 17.3 points per game. In 2000,

Below, Sheryl helps lead the Comets to victory in the WNBA finals, August 26, 2000.

Sheryl Swoopes (front) parades with team to celebrate their win over Australia at the 2000 Olympic Games.

she was named the league's Most Valuable Player and the defensive player of the year, and was the leading vote-getter for the 2000 all-star game! So what did Sheryl do for an encore after having won just about every possible award in the sport? How about winning a second gold medal as a member of the 2000 U.S. Olympic basketball team that stormed to victory in Sydney, Australia!

Sheryl, along with many other hard-working women basketball players, helped change the shape of the sport forever. Once relegated to the sidelines, girls who play basketball now have many goals they can aspire to. Sheryl helps to encourage these aspirations by conducting basketball camps where girls get careful attention from experienced coaches.

In addition, she appears in many commercials. Companies love her outgoing, happy personality. And they know that her success has come from a lot of hard work and dedication that helped her overcome obstacles. That creates a positive image both for their company and for women's athletics.

There just doesn't seem to be anything Sheryl Swoopes cannot do.

Sheryl, along with several other hard-working women basketball players, helped change the shape of the sport forever.

Chronology

- 1971, born on March 25.
- 1988, leads Brownfield High School to Texas state championship.
- 1989, enrolls at South Plains Community College.
- 1991, is named Junior College Player of the Year.
- 1993, leads the Texas Tech Lady Raiders to the NCAA championship.
- 1995, becomes the first woman athlete to have a shoe named after her as Nike introduces the Air Swoopes.
- 1996, helps the U.S. win Olympic basketball gold medal.
- 1997, gives birth to son Jordan.
- 1997, signs with the Houston Comets of the WNBA.
- 2000, named Most Valuable Player of the WNBA.
- 2000, wins second gold medal as member of Women's Olympic basketball team.

Index